Mark Sanchez

by **Michael Sandler**

Consultant: James Alder
Football Expert
football.about.com

PUBLISHING

New York, New York

Credits

Cover and Title Page, © John Dunn/MCT/Landov and AP Photo/Bill Kostroun; 4, © Matt Campbell/EPA/Landov; 5, © AP Photo/Stephan Savoia; 6, © Al Bello/Getty Images; 7, © Elsa/Getty Images; 8, © The Sanchez family/Landov; 9, © Marin Media/Cal Sport Media/ZUMA Press/Newscom; 10, © Jim Ruymen/UPI/Landov; 11, © AP Photo/Rich Schultz; 12, © John Angelillo/UPI/Landov; 13, © AP Photo/Kevin Terrell; 14, © Icon SMI/Newscom; 15, © David Bergman/Sports Illustrated/Getty Images; 16, © Hollenbeck Youth Center; 17T, © Hollenbeck Youth Center/Photo by Eric A. Van Dyke, Inner-City Games Photographer; 17B, © Hollenbeck Youth Center/Inner-City Games Los Angeles; 18, © Mike Young/Juvenile Diabetes Research Foundation (JDRF); 19, © AP Photo/Mel Evans; 20, © AP Photo/Bill Kostroun; 21, © Mike Segar/Reuters/Landov; 22L, © KRT/Newscom; 22R, © Brooks Van Arx/ZUMA Press/Newscom.

Publisher: Kenn Goin
Senior Editor: Lisa Wiseman
Creative Director: Spencer Brinker
Photo Researcher: Picture Perfect Professionals, LLC
Design: Dawn Beard Creative

Library of Congress Cataloging-in-Publication Data

Sandler, Michael, 1965–
  Mark Sanchez / by Michael Sandler.
      p. cm. — (Football heroes making a difference)
  Includes bibliographical references and index.
  ISBN-13: 978-1-61772-310-0 (library binding)
  ISBN-10: 1-61772-310-X (library binding)
  1. Sanchez, Mark—Juvenile literature. 2. Football players—United States—Biography—Juvenile literature. 3. Quarterbacks (Football)—United States—Biography—Juvenile literature. I. Title.
  GV939.S175S26 2012
  796.332092—dc22
  [B]
                                        2011007784

For more information, write to Bearport Publishing Company, Inc., 45 West 21st Street, Suite 3B, New York, New York 10010. Printed in the United States of America in North Mankato, Minnesota.

070111
042711CGC

10 9 8 7 6 5 4 3 2 1

CONTENTS

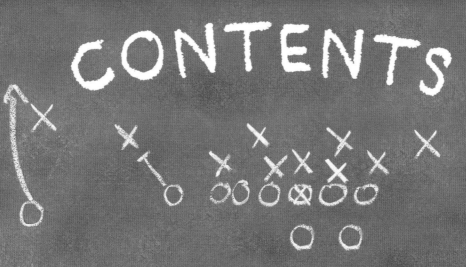

Impossible

It was January 16, 2011, and Mark Sanchez was playing in the biggest game of his newly-begun NFL career. The young quarterback and his team, the New York Jets, were facing **All-Pro** quarterback Tom Brady and the New England Patriots. The winner would move on to the 2010–2011 **AFC Championship Game**.

Most sports fans were certain that the Patriots would win. After all, just a few weeks earlier, they had crushed the Jets, 45–3. No one seemed to think that New York had a chance—except for the Jets players themselves.

For Mark, being the **underdog** was just extra **motivation**. "When somebody tells you you can't," Mark would say later, "all you want to do is prove them wrong."

Mark sits on the sideline after throwing his second interception of the December 6, 2010, game.

In the loss to the Patriots on December 6, 2010, Mark had not played his best—throwing three **interceptions**. Tom Brady, on the other hand, was unstoppable. He threw four touchdown passes without getting **picked off** once.

Mark gets ready to throw the ball in the January 16, 2011, game against the New England Patriots.

Victory in New England

"Prove them wrong" is just what Mark and the Jets did. Patriots fans quickly grew silent watching the **ferocious** Jets defense pressure Tom Brady. Finding open **receivers** proved impossible for the Patriots quarterback.

Mark, on the other hand, completed pass after pass, including second-quarter touchdown throws to LaDainian Tomlinson and Braylon Edwards. By halftime, New York held a 14–3 lead.

Later in the game, when New England threatened a comeback, Mark came through again. In the fourth quarter, he spotted Santonio Holmes and threw him the ball for yet another touchdown. At game's end, the impossible had happened. The Jets had beaten the Patriots, 28–21.

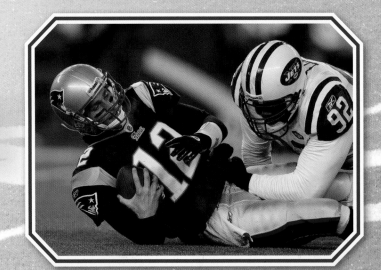

Tom Brady (#12) gets sacked.

Mark (#6) looks to hand off the ball during the game against the Patriots.

Mark completed 16 out of 25 passes without an interception, and threw for 194 yards (177 m) in the Jets' victory over New England.

Learning the Game

Mark's journey to NFL glory began as a child in Mission Viejo, California. Growing up, he dreamed about becoming a pro quarterback. His bedroom walls were covered with posters of star NFL passers such as the Houston Oilers' Warren Moon and the Miami Dolphins' Dan Marino.

Mark learned to play football from his father and his two older brothers, Brandon and Nick. His dad, Nick Sr., was a firefighter who had once been a high school quarterback. Nick Sr. spent hours with his son teaching him the game and practicing passing in the park. Often the pair stayed out late, long after the sun went down. Only the headlights from the family pickup truck made it possible for them to keep playing.

Mark playing football as a child

Mark (#6) playing quarterback for Mission Viejo High School in 2004

Mark's long hours of practice paid off in high school. He became the football team's star quarterback and one of the highest-rated high school passers in the entire country.

From USC to the NFL

Dozens of colleges wanted Mark to come play for them. Despite many options, Mark chose to stay close to home and went to the University of Southern California (USC). The school's football team, the USC Trojans, already had several strong quarterbacks with more experience than Mark. He wasn't given many chances to play until his fourth year. It was then that he became the team's **starter**, and he made the most of the opportunity.

In 2008, he helped the Trojans win 12 out of 13 games, impressing everyone with his energy, leadership, and accurate passing. By the season's end, many NFL teams wanted Mark to play for them. The New York Jets were the lucky team, choosing Mark with the fifth pick in the 2009 NFL **draft**.

Mark (#6) celebrates with his USC teammates after throwing a touchdown pass in the 2009 Rose Bowl.

New York Jets owner Woody Johnson (left) presents Mark (right) with a Jets jersey.

Mark saved his best performance for his final game at USC, a meeting with Penn State in the 2009 **Rose Bowl**. Mark passed for four touchdowns and 413 yards (378 m), his career best at the school. Afterward, he was named the Rose Bowl **MVP**.

A Coach's Trust

Rookies usually need time to get used to playing in the NFL, so most coaches don't have them play a lot at first. The Jets' coach, Rex Ryan, however, believed in Mark from the start. On Mark's first NFL play, in a preseason game against the St. Louis Rams, Coach Ryan called for a difficult, deep pass. Mark met Coach Ryan's challenge by making a perfect 48-yard (44-m) throw.

Impressed by Mark's **poise**, Coach Ryan named him as starter when the 2009–2010 regular season began. Mark rewarded Coach Ryan's trust by helping the Jets to three straight wins.

Although Mark played well, he did have his ups and downs as the season went on. Sometimes he threw too quickly, not waiting for receivers to get open. Sometimes he threw bad passes that ended up as interceptions. All in all, however, Mark had an incredible rookie season.

Mark (left) stands on the sideline near Coach Ryan (right) during a preseason game in 2009.

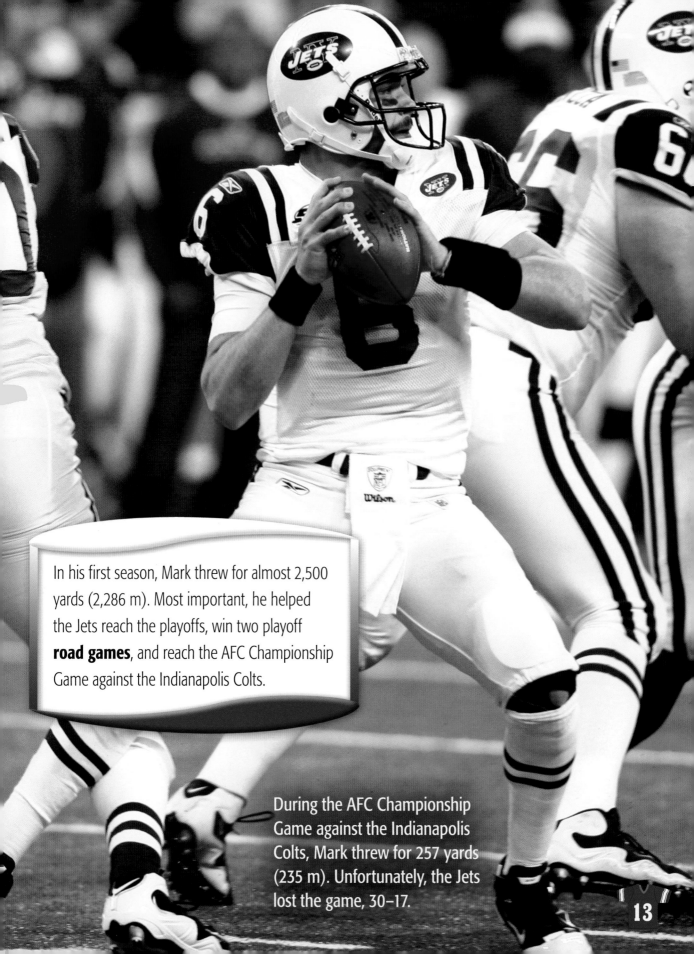

In his first season, Mark threw for almost 2,500 yards (2,286 m). Most important, he helped the Jets reach the playoffs, win two playoff **road games**, and reach the AFC Championship Game against the Indianapolis Colts.

During the AFC Championship Game against the Indianapolis Colts, Mark threw for 257 yards (235 m). Unfortunately, the Jets lost the game, 30–17.

Even Better

After his first season, Mark worked hard at improving his skills. He spent weeks practicing and watching **game film**. The long hours Mark spent training paid off during the 2010–2011 season. He threw five more touchdowns and seven fewer interceptions than he had the previous year. New York finished with an 11–5 record.

The Jets returned to the playoffs and upset two **favored** teams while winning on the road. First, they beat the Indianapolis Colts, 17–16. Then Mark and the Jets came away with an incredible 28–21 win over the New England Patriots. Jets fans will always remember Mark's outstanding play in New York's shocking **upset**.

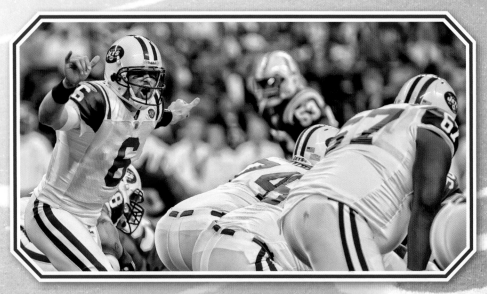

Mark (#6) calls out a play during the January 8, 2011, win against the Colts.

Mark's hard work helped the Jets upset the Patriots 28–21 on January 16, 2011.

Before Mark, no Jets quarterback had ever led his team to four playoff victories in his first two years in the league.

Working Harder

Football isn't the only thing that Mark works hard at. He also works hard at helping kids. One way he shows his support is by giving back to the Hollenbeck Youth Center, a group that organizes athletic, educational, and cultural programs to help children stay out of trouble.

One of the youth center's winter activities is a holiday toy drive. The center provides thousands of Christmas gifts to kids in the Los Angeles area. Mark first began volunteering with the group while he was a student at USC. "I would go over to the toy drive around Christmastime because I didn't have money back then and I would donate my time." As an NFL player, Mark still works with the center, serving as a **spokesperson** to help others learn about its **mission**, as well as raising money for the group.

Kids from the Hollenbeck Youth Center practice karate.

Mark poses with some of the Inner-City
Games basketball players in 2010.

Mark and a young Inner-City
Games athlete

Each year, the Hollenbeck Youth Center
runs the Los Angeles Inner-City Games,
which gives more than 40,000 kids
in the Los Angeles area the chance to
compete in sports such as swimming,
football, softball, and basketball.

Fighting Diabetes

Another way Mark helps kids is by joining in the fight against juvenile diabetes, a serious disease that affects the way the body processes sugar. While there is no cure for the illness, treatments can help people with diabetes live normal lives. Juvenile diabetes is usually found in children, teens, and young adults.

To show his support, Mark works with the Juvenile Diabetes Research Foundation (JDRF). In 2010, he competed in an online contest against other NFL players to win a $100,000 **grant** for the organization. Though he didn't win the contest, he was awarded $25,000 to be used by the JDRF to create programs to help spread the word about the importance of **diagnosing** juvenile diabetes early on.

To raise money for diabetes research, the JDRF holds a walk every year.

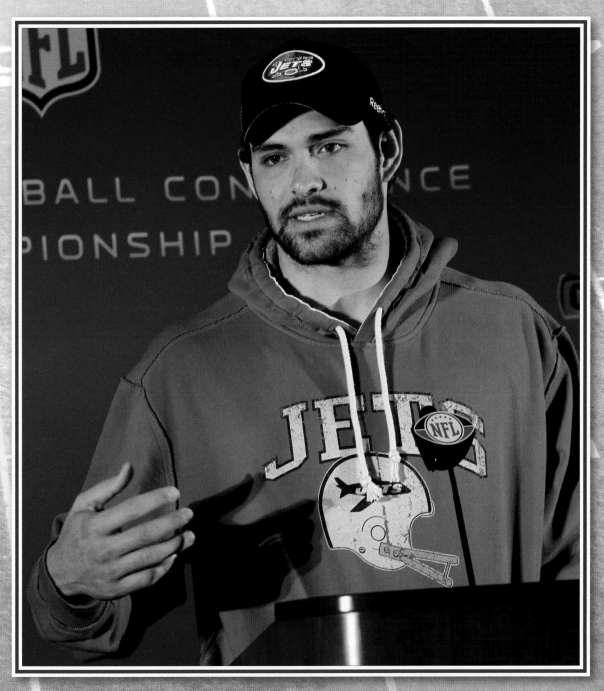

If warning signs for diabetes are found early on, then treatment can be provided quickly—before the disease becomes life threatening.

To try to win the $100,000 grant, Mark made a television appearance and spoke on the radio about his support for the JDRF.

Into the Future

Mark Sanchez has already earned himself a place as one of football's best young passers. He's only the second quarterback in NFL history to reach a conference championship game in each of his first two seasons.

Jets fans have high hopes that Mark will soon take the team even further—all the way to the Super Bowl. No one can predict just how much success Mark will achieve in years to come. One thing is certain, however: Mark will continue his hard work on and off the field, helping both his teammates and the kids whom he cares about.

Mark with some of his fans

Mark has already won four playoff road games as a starting quarterback. That's more than quarterback greats such as Dan Marino and Brett Favre accomplished in their entire football careers.

21

The Mark File

Mark is a hero both on and off the field. Here are some highlights.

In December 2010, as the Jets' regular season was winding down, Mark heard about an 11-year-old boy named Aiden Binkley who wanted to meet him. Aiden was suffering from a rare disease. Mark and his teammates brought Aiden to the Jets' training facility, where he got to meet the players and watch the team practice. Mark and Aiden became friends, keeping in touch during the last few weeks of the boy's life.

On November 7, 2010, Mark threw for 336 yards (307 m) in a game against the Detroit Lions. It marked his career high with the Jets and was his first 300-yard (274-m) game.

If Mark ends up leading New York all the way to the Super Bowl, he will become the first Jets quarterback to do so since Joe Namath back in 1969.

Glossary

AFC Championship Game (AY-EFF-SEE CHAM-pee-uhn-*ship* GAME) a playoff game that decides which American Football Conference (AFC) team will go to the Super Bowl

All-Pro (*awl*-PROH) a player who is voted one of the best in the league at his position

diagnosing (*dye*-uhg-NOHS-ing) finding out the cause of a person's medical problems

draft (DRAFT) an event in which pro teams take turns choosing college players to play for them

favored (FAY-vurd) expected to win

ferocious (fuh-ROH-shuhss) fierce and unstoppable

game film (GAME FILM) recordings of games already played; used by players to study the skills and strategies of their opponents

grant (GRANT) money given by a group to another group to use for a special purpose

interceptions (*in*-tur-SEP-shuhnz) passes that are caught by players on the defensive team

mission (MISH-uhn) a certain job or task to be performed

motivation (*moh*-tuh-VAY-shuhn) the ability to encourage someone to do something

MVP (EM-VEE-PEE) the most valuable player

picked off (PIKT AWF) being intercepted; having a ball meant for a receiver caught by a player from the other team

poise (POIZ) the ability to stay cool and calm

receivers (ri-SEE-vurz) players whose job it is to catch passes

road games (ROHD GAMEZ) games played away from home, at the other team's stadium

rookies (RUK-eez) first-year players

Rose Bowl (ROHZ BOHL) a famous college football game held each year in Pasadena, California

spokesperson (SPOHKS-*pur*-suhn) a person who represents a company or organization

starter (START-ur) a person who plays at the start of a game; the best player at a position

underdog (UHN-dur-*dawg*) an athlete or team not expected to win

upset (UHP-set) a game won by a team that was expected to lose

Bibliography

The New York Times

USA Today

Hispanicbusiness.com

NFL.com

Read More

Goodman, Michael E. *The Story of the New York Jets.* Mankato, MN: Creative Education (2009).

Sandler, Michael. *Pro Football's Most Spectacular Quarterbacks (Football-O-Rama).* New York: Bearport (2011).

Williams, Zella. *Mark Sanchez: Quarterbacks on the Rise.* New York: PowerKids Press (2011).

Learn More Online

To learn more about Mark Sanchez and the New York Jets, visit
www.bearportpublishing.com/FootballHeroes

Index

24